HARRY THOMAS'
MEMORY LANE
VOLUME IV

RHYL PRESTATYN
VISITOR

A COLLECTION OF HARRY'S PICTURES & STORIES FROM HIS
RHYL & PRESTATYN VISITOR NEWSPAPER COLUMN, MEMORY LANE

Also available: Harry Thomas' Memory Lane, Volumes I, II & III
More local history books available at: www.gwasg.com

ISBN: 978-09550338-6-5
© Printed & Published in November 2006
by Gwasg Helygain Ltd
68/70 Kinmel Street, Rhyl, Denbighshire LL18 1AW
Tel: 01745 331411 Fax: 01745 331310
info@gwasg.com www.gwasg.com

Introduction

Since writing the very first Memory Lane column for the Rhyl & Prestatyn Visitor newspaper way back in October 2002 after being requested by their Production Editor Mark Jones, who originated this prestigious local history column, little did I realise that the subsequent years would see the publication of three books and that I would be writing this introduction for my fourth Memory Lane book.

When my writing appeared each week in The Visitor I feared that once the local history features had appeared in that week's paper that they were in jeopardy of being lost in the vast numbers of back issues of newspapers, never to see the light of day again. This gave me the idea of publishing each year's Memory Lane column in book form for readers and local history enthusiasts to enjoy once again that magical history tour through their community, and possibly be of value to future historians, schools and local history groups to delve into.

From the comments I receive from the readers and the people I meet every day, I find that the majority of you tend to cut out and keep the Memory Lane page and pass them on to relatives and friends who once lived in the locality. Subsequently those friends and relatives of Memory Lane readers have in turn, very thoughtfully, sent me some very engaging stories complemented with photographs relating to Rhyl, Prestatyn and neighbourhood which in turn have been recounted here and in previous Volumes of Memory Lane.

I have discovered that since I began the Memory Lane column there are many of you in the 'golden ages' of your lives that have numerous fascinating and colourful treasured memories relating to the town or village where you were born and bred, and it has been thoroughly delightful and enlightening over the years to have met and conversed with many of you.

The endearing memories of Dorothy Chard of Prestatyn, who, during my conversations with her recalled and brought vividly to life the clearest of memories when as a young girl along with her sister she used to watch The Prestos entertainment troupe on the beach at Prestatyn during the 1930s. And the four Rhyl girls who conversed with John Lennon and Paul McCartney when they saw The Beatles play at Prestatyn's Royal Lido in 1962.

Also the wonderful ninety year old Muriel Smythe who told me of her days when she and her husband ran the Woodlands Restaurant and Bungalow Garage along Gwespyr's Coast Road for many years. All these stories, and more, are featured in the pages of this book.

I trust that the local history stories within this book will linger long in the memory as they have for me, and will make you think of so much that was good that has now gone. To protect our future we must learn from the past - but do we ever? Happy days!

Harry Thomas

November 2006

I am continually looking for additions to my archive and would be interested in purchasing all types of old picture postcards, old local china, souvenir items, local cine film and also viewing or copying items of local interest. If you have anything that might be of interest please don't hesitate to call me on 01745 - 889773.

Foreword

RHYL PRESTATYN VISITOR

It is astonishing to think that we have reached volume four of Harry Thomas's Memory Lane compilations, culled from his regular columns in the Rhyl, Prestatyn and Abergele Visitor newspaper.

It hardly seems five minutes since volume one made its debut at a launch in the surroundings of Boswell's cafe bar on Bodfor Street in Rhyl.

The march of time often subtly alters the way we live and our surroundings and in the early part of the new millennium we are seeing increasing and major change to the townscapes of Rhyl and Prestatyn, hence the need for people like Harry to chronicle the way life used to be and the faces and places that are now long gone.

Memory Lane remains one of the best-read and best-loved features in the Visitor and it is remarkable that Harry always turns up something new to enchant his readers week in, week out.

I know from talking to our readership that the column often brings great joy to older residents of the area who see nostalgic pictures of their old homes, schools, workplaces, pubs they used to frequent or fields they played in as children.

And this is the whole point of nostalgia, not only to record for posterity the passing of time, but to invoke a warmth and affection for that one thing we can never bring back, the past.

Over the years Harry has become a master of this art, mixing minute detail in with (often rose-tinted) affection for a time when life was slower, less cluttered by the rigours of this technological age, and people went about their business with a more sedate air, unhurried by the pressures of time and the stresses that seem to weigh upon this modern age.

The Visitor is delighted to provide a platform for Harry's work and I know that his loyal readership looks forward to what is fast becoming a regular fixture in the pre-Christmas build-up, the launch of the latest volume of Memory Lane compilations.

As a company, we are delighted to be associated with this project which is so skilfully put together by Guto, family and staff at Gwasg Helygain and we all look forward to next year when, no doubt, Harry will be putting the finishing touches to volume five of Memory Lane.

Mark Jones
Production Editor
Visitor/Vale Series Newspapers
Llandudno Junction
November 2006

Acknowledgments

I am indebted and more than greatful to the following for their more than generous contributions and for those of you who had to endure my harassment during the compilation of this book; the directors of Gwasg Helygain Ltd, Eddie, Linda, Sian & Guto Lloyd-Davies for their enthusiastic, invaluable and ceaseless support in the publishing of this book; Fred Hobbs, June Tynan, Vivien Hughes Davies, Dorothy Chard, Richard Jones, Karen Lloyd, Peter & Rhiannon Robinson, Tom Parry, Gill Evans, Prestatyn and Rhyl Libraries, Philip Smith, Michael Lewis-Jones, Dave Kenny, Muriel Smythe, Jo Talbot, Donna Blythin, Helen Rowe, Jessica Batty, Jenny Walker, Hazel Walker & James Ouslem.

This book is dedicated to those most treasured in my life: Emma Thomas & Harry Thomas Jnr.

Harry Thomas
November 2006

Contents

Old Cinema Days

Visiting the local cinema in your youth when the heroes in the films were cheered and the villains hissed and booed is for many of you a lasting experience that is held with deep affection. But nobody holds those endearing memories more than the people in the close knit community of Mostyn.

Films were first shown in the church hall at Mostyn for many years by Ted Parry and later at his wooden hut fondly known as TP's (or more often the laugh and scratch) located behind the *"squares"* - 45 terraced houses set well back from the Coast Road and vacated 1969 for more suitable housing at Maes Pennant.

Morgan Freight today occupies land where the Squares once stood. At TP's you were assured of a cheap nights entertainment, unlike today's widescreen, comfortably seated, air conditioned and heated cinemas. Seating at TP's consisted of old sofas and benches and not many objected to the discomfort once the picture started.

Films were always pre war offerings and even in the late 1940s you could expect to see one silent film at an evening's show. The favourites were Laurel and Hardy, Rin Tin Tin, Charlie Chan and in later years the films of Abbott and Costello, The Three Stooges and a Mickey Mouse cartoon. Admission to TP's was six pence (3p) for adults and then three pence (1 1/2p) for children. The little boy who took the admission on the door was Tom Parry (Ted's son) who grew up to become head master of Bodnant School, Prestatyn from 1960 to 1989 and was subsequently chairman of Denbighshire County Council from 2003-04.

During the interval a cup of tea and a piece of cake for tuppence (1p) was served. And the noise was deafening when the film broke, as it often did.

When the film had been rethreaded and the audience had settled down to see the end of the picture, what an uproar there was when everyone sitting on the sofas and benches realised that the film had been fed into the projector upside down, which of course gave added excitement for another night to remember at TP's.

During the 1950s film shows were started at the iron works canteen. The films were very much of the same vintage as shown at TP's but the sheer luxury of the canteen seats and well lit warm premises, with no roof leaks and fewer spiders and mice made the film shows at the iron works very popular. In addition Lyons ice cream could be bought which came in round slices wrapped in soft card.

The curtains have long since drawn on showing films at Mostyn. Ted Parry's hut ended its days as a stable for horses and the iron works canteen was demolished during dockside development.

Top photo: The Squares Mostyn pictured in the early 1950s
Bottom photo: The men of the Squares with T.P.'s hut in the background in 1953. The little boy in the front is Tom Parry and Ted is seen wearing the white shirt and braces.

Great love affair with rail travel

Built at a cost of £1,113 Prestatyn's original railway station, which stands in station yard at the bottom of the town, is an evocative 150-year-old reminder of the embryonic days of rail travel and the town's development as a thriving and popular seaside resort. Opened on May 1, 1848, when the population of Prestatyn was 250 (population for the 2001 census was 18,496) and today under a preservation order through support from myself, it is the only one of four surviving stone built stations of its kind designed by Chester to Holyhead Railway architect, Francis Thompson. Prestatyn being the finest and best surviving example of his work.

With the advent of rail travel, the gateway to North Wales was opened to the vast number of people eager to visit the seaside resorts along the North Wales coast (the coach and horse was the previous mode of transport which only the wealthy could afford).
By the late 1800s, Prestatyn's original railway station echoed to the sounds of excitement and merriment of the vast numbers of adults and children who arrived at Prestatyn (as they still do today) for their holiday's. Longing to escape the noise and smoke-filled industrial towns and cites of the North and Midlands, all wound-up like clockwork toys ready to unwind for the week or day away, to wallow in the sea, take in the salubrious ozone-filled air and tread Prestatyn's lengthy beach.

The popularity, prosperity and growth of Prestatyn as a seaside resort grew rapidly in those early years and a great love affair with rail travel to Prestatyn remained a favourite destination, with the town's very first railway station playing a valuable and important role. In its heyday, the station had two platforms with a small footbridge, which extended over the rails for passengers to cross.

One drawback to the old station was the level of the platforms. They were too low for passengers alighting and a special ladder had to be used causing

delay and inconvenience as it had to be moved several times as passengers stepped off the train.

The platforms were also too short, resulting in numerous accidents. The outcome was that when a train of extra length drew up to the platforms passengers had difficulty in getting off. The old station was replaced in 1897 by a more modern and larger station which is still in use today.

The present railway station building was modernised in 1971. Today, the 150-year-old station building at the bottom of Prestatyn High Street stands as a superb monument to the beginnings of rail travel and the growth of the tourist industry in Prestatyn.

Opposite Page: Prestatyn's original railway station pictured in 1890.
Above: Vast numbers from the North and and Midlands descend on Prestatyn Station for their holidays in 1909. This station was built in 1879 and then modernised and enlarged in 1971. It replaced the older building which can still be seen today in Station Yard at the bottom of the High Street.

The golden era

With the untimely demise of Rhyl's once much-loved illustrious crowd-pulling attractions; the Pier, Floral Hall, outdoor swimming pool, Marine Lake, Ocean Beach Fun Fair, Pavilion, Gaiety and Coliseum Theatres, the Botanical and Coronation Gardens along Grange Road are the last vestige left over from Rhyl's *"golden era"*, and are today an invaluable asset to the town.

The Botanical Gardens were developed in 1928 by Rhyl Urban District Council in the midst of an economic depression as a place of recreation for visitors and the people of Rhyl. The Coronation Gardens behind the Botanical Gardens were developed nine years later in 1936.

A 1930s holiday guide to Rhyl, which describes the Botanical Gardens, is an evocative read and appropriate today: *"The Botanical Gardens attract admiration to visitors and locals alike where the beauties of nature are set.*

"The extensive gardens situated in the Grange Road present not only a delight to the eye but means of recreation and leisure which is hardly equalled in any other resort.

"There is a beautiful pavilion and café constructed in Italian style, and the rose garden is an explosion of hundreds of blooms distilling their fragrance in the summer air. In the confines of the garden are 12 tennis courts, a miniature golf course and a crown green bowling green.

"Passing through the entrance over-strung with roses, visitors can wander among the flowers or proceed to the sports centre as ample provision is made for tennis and bowls.

"The garden's café provides one with the most

welcome cup of tea. The ponds in the gardens must be seen as they are a riot of colour from early spring to autumn."

In August 2004, the Rhyl South West Central Residents Group incorporating Save the Botanical Gardens was formed as a result of campaigning against the proposed relocation by the County Council of the Births, Deaths and Marriages Office from Rhyl town centre to the café in the centre of the gardens which the County Council closed in 2003, and meant cutting down very old and rare trees in the gardens to create a car park.

A petition totalling 2,400 signatures opposing the move was a success through sheer determination of the local residents, and consequently the County Council reconsidered and relocated elsewhere.

Today the café is open seven days a week, staffed by volunteers and has become a community centre for meetings by Rhyl Swimming Club, Rhyl Tennis Club, Rhyl's over-50s Club, Rhyl's Townswomen's Guild and surgeries for the Police and AM Ann Jones. What was previously a derelict facility, has today become a thriving centre for the young and old.

I was given a personal tour of the gardens by the knowledgeable and committed George Owen, president of the Residents Group, it was jaw-dropping to see the vastness of the gardens in what was an explosion of colour in an oasis of tranquillity in the heart of Rhyl. A coffee at the café complemented an enjoyable experience and I thank George for his valuable time. Why visit the Chelsea Flower Show!

Opposite page: Botanical Gardens, Café and Bowling Green pictured in the 1940s.
Above: The Botanical Gardens's colourful pergolas over-strung with roses. One of the must-see attractions in the gardens, pictured here in the 1940s.

Fond memories of Auntie May

Inset in a wall in the community garden adjoining the side of the Gronant Inn, is a plaque dedicated to the memory of one of Gronant's much loved characters May Owen, who for many years, ran a small wooden shop where the community garden is today.

Although disabled from birth and permanently confined to her wheelchair, May had the strength of character and determination to run her own shop selling sweets, cigarettes, fruit and vegetables. May would be seen manoeuvring her heavy wooden wheelchair around the two counters of her shop with the dexterity of a younger woman. She kept herself warm in her cold shop during the winter by making cups of tea from the kettle that sat on top of the valor paraffin stove that kept her shop warm.

May wore her long brown hair parted in the middle and plaited on either side. Her hair was so long that she could sit on it. Her next door neighbour recalls that she would wash it on Thursday afternoons (early closing at the shop) and if it was a warm sunny day she would sit in the back garden running her fingers through her hair in the sunshine.

May's many friends were more than happy to volunteer to push her along the rough track to and from her home at 2 Maes y Dre and that certainly needed strength. May's devoted father often pushed her to the shops at Prestatyn or to Llanasa Church, accompanied by her little dog Lady who waited outside. During the First World War when cigarettes were in short supply her shop was broken into several times, sometimes by soldiers from the camps at Prestatyn. May became good friends with many of the residents in Gronant who would often drop into her shop for a chat and advice; she was a trusted confidant who seemed to bring out the gentleness in the worst of characters. The old and young called her 'Auntie May'. She knitted baby clothes for every new baby in the village from patterns in Home Chat and Women's Weekly. Later in life she enjoyed a battery-powered wheelchair which meant for the first time in her life she could go out unaccompanied.

When St Winifred's Church came into use in Gronant she became a regular attender and later a Sunday school teacher there, making and selling items in aid of church funds.

The landlord of the Gronant Inn is constantly reminded of May Owen's memory by the stories of her life in the village told by many local customers.

The erection of a plaque by the residents of Gronant where her shop once stood is a dedication to Auntie May's memory, who always had a kind word and smile for everyone. Photograph of May Owen courtesy of Vic and Hilda Parry.

Looking back at the best days of our lives

A picture gallery of old school photographs continually delights and holds considerable interest and charm for readers of the Memory Lane column. And for those of you who take great pleasure in recognising old school friends, here is another selection of old school photographs for your scrutiny. We wonder where they all are now!

The photograph above is of Prestatyn Clawdd Offa School in the 1960s. Back row, standing from left to right, are: Brian Lewis, Vernon Egerton-Jones and Phil Williams. Back row sitting L-R: David Evans, David Owen, Tony Allitt, Peter Gregory, Kenny Stevens, RC Jones, David P Owen, Brian Holmes and Phil Stanly.

Front row sitting L-R: Clive Morris, Noel Cambell, David Hughes, Michael Holiday, Martin Lodge, Stuart Maybury, Philip Wharton Lumsden, Brian Jones.

Clawdd Offa School opened on August 30th 1956. The first headmaster at the school was Dan Owen, and the school was designed for 620 pupils. When it opened on the Tuesday it was said to be already overcrowded. Today the old Clawdd Offa is known as Prestatyn High School.

The photograph above was kindly donated by Gwen Owen of Penyffordd and is of Ffynnongroyw CP infants school, Mornant Avenue, pictured in 1948.

Back row L-R: teacher Miss Jones, Gwyn?, Gwynn Jones, Alan Harrison, Raymond Parry, Raymond Williams, Edmund Roberts (passed away in 2001), Tommy Owens (known as *"chips"*, parents ran the chip shop in the village).
Middle row L-R: unknown, unknown, Glyn Thomas, Edith Jones, Eirlys Thomas, Dorothy Latham.
Front row L-R, Maureen Stockton, Pamela Dennis, Margaret Davies, Rita Parry, Eirwen Parry, Gwen Roberts, Nan Jones (passed away in 2003).

In those days, due to lack of space, the school children at Ffynnongroyw CP Infants had to walk to Moriah Chapel Schoolroom at the other end of the village for their school dinners.

Happiest days?

We look back at the best days of our lives in a picture gallery of school photographs, which is always a popular feature with Memory Lane readers, and holds considerable interest and pleasure for those of you who take great delight in identifying old school friends, relatives and loved ones. The top photograph is of Gwespyr Picton School, pictured in the 1960s.

Back row L-R, Andrew Males, Vincent Price, Chris Price, Martin Jones, Teacher Miss Williams
Middle row L-R Yvonne Morris, Sylvia Roberts, Sheila Faulkner, Shirley Wilson,
Front row L-R, Graham Jones, Dawn Kenny, Rea Hughes, Ellie Begley, Gwilym Cook.

Famous actor, author and playwright Emlyn Williams was one of the first pupils to attend Picton School when it first opened in 1914. At the time he was living at the White Lion Inn, Glan-yr-Afon. Owned by his father Richard.

In 1938 Emlyn Williams wrote the best selling book The Corn is Green, about his life in Welsh mining community. It later became a film classic starring Bette Davies. Emlyn Williams died at his London home in 1987 (see page 22 of my book Memory Lane Volume I).

I myself attended Picton and one of my lasting memories of the school was that during playtime in the summer one of the kitchen staff rang a bell at the door of the canteen calling out "ice" and we would all run to be given an ice cube to cool us in the heat of the day.

It was a small miracle as children that none of us choked on those large chunks of ice.

This photograph is a Abergele Grammar School First Eleven hockey team 1955-56 season after winning the North Wales cup.

Back row L-R, Glenys Oliver, Angela Hewitt, Hilary Owen, unknown, Miss Beardmore.
Middle row L-R, Betty Jones, Gaynor Lloyd Jones, Eirlys Williams, unknown, unknown.
Front row L-R, Myra Lloyd Jones, Unknown.

The craze that swept Britain

Roller blading and skate boarding are modern activities enjoyed by all ages today and owe their discovery and design to the roller skate patented by Jones Plimpton of New York in 1863. The roller skating craze swept Britain in the late 1860s and although roller skating continued to have its devoted followers, it lingered on with diminishing popularity over the succeeding years. Despite the diminishing popularity of roller skating during those early years, "rinking" on large smooth marble floors in established skating rinks in the 1900s was still enjoyed by the majority of the public as one of the more enjoyable pastimes of the day, although the skating craze had been and gone.

Nevertheless, observers in public entertainment throughout the country, which included Rhyl, were confident that the roller skating craze was going to make a comeback.

On the strength of this, Rhyl opened its new roller skating rink at the Queen's on July 27 1908, only eight months after the disastrous fire which destroyed the famous Queen's Palace Roof Gardens and the Arcade shopping centre. (See page 25 of my book Memory Lane Vol I).

The new rink floor was made of marble and covered 4,000 feet and was 180 feet in length, the main entrance to the new skating rink was from the promenade (where the entrance from the promenade to the indoor market is today, near the Queen's Bowling Arcade). The exit ran into Sussex Street (today's entrance to the indoor market from Sussex Street) above the entrance can still be seen the words *"Queen's Arcade AD 1902"*.

An elegant insight into the Queen's skating rink comes from a 1908 advert – *"Only the best Winslow ball-bearings skates are in use and in addition to ordinary skating there will be fancy and trick exhibitions performed by E. Velosky. Music will be played by the Military Band performances at 2.30pm and 7.30pm"*.

In later years, Rhyl's Queens skating rink formed its own roller skating hockey team (pictured above in 1912). Roller skating made a brief revival during the 1950s and 60s and for a short time a popular outdoor roller skating rink was established on Rhyl's promenade.

Guto Lloyd-Davies, of Memory Lane's publishers Gwasg Helygain, remembers the promenade skating rink all too well. In the summer of 1987, aged 13, he'd gone skating there with his cousin Dafydd Wilkinson, but fell breaking both bones in his right arm. He was taken to the Red Cross Nurse's Office (and Lost Children's Office) next door where he had an anxious wait for his parents to take him to hospital. In those days, minor injuries and lost children were all attended to in that office on the promenade.

The rink was eventually demolished to make way for the controversial Children's Village in the early 1990s.

Opposite page: The Queen's Roller Skating Rink and a small crowd of roller skating enthusiasts pose for this delightful photo in 1913.

Bygone days of old Prestatyn

The top postcard, that certainly lingers long in memory, is one of the more alluring and delightful postcards of Prestatyn from my archives as it speaks volumes and is an invaluable and evocative insight into a bygone age of the small town atmosphere of Prestatyn. Endearingly captured in this turn-of-the-century posed-for photograph looking down the town's High Street in 1911 from today's J Jones Furniture and Upholsterers shop (formerly E B Jones the grocers, the name which can still be seen in the tiled doorway of the shop). Before Rehoboth Church was built and extended in 1894 (pictured on the right), members of this church were said to be worshipping in a small chapel in Fforddlas in 1823. Today the old chapel building is a private residence known as Plas Ifan. The four young girls pictured here were no doubt visiting the sweet shop located, during the early years, alongside the church and owned by Mary Thomas who was well-known in the town for her home-made treacle toffee and ginger beer.

The whitewashed cottages on the right were known as Pendre Cottages. Grenville Williams came into possession of these cottages in 1880, his great-uncle Edward Jones subsequently purchased these cottages when he was a policeman in the town.

During the late 1800s when Prestatyn was still a village with a population of only 700 (2001 census 18,496) there wasn't a police station in Prestatyn and the only village constable lived at the end of Pendre Cottages. Prestatyn's very first police station was built in Nant Hall Road in 1903 (today Citizens Advice Bureau). Ann Ellis, one of the residents of Pendre Cottages had the most graceful singing voice in Prestatyn and called in her son Pugh when out playing by singing his name. Her dulcet tones were said to be heard throughout the High Street. Pugh lost his life as a soldier during the First World War. Pendre Cottages, the last vestiges of old Prestatyn, were demolished in 1958.

Freeland's grocers on the left was owned by a Mr Edward Jones and when he first opened, he placed a sign in his shop window saying *"Lookout Jones Freeland stores opening soon"*.

From then on he was known in the town as *"Jones Lookout"*. The two stone gate posts to the shops house on the left below the sign can still be seen in place there today.

The bottom photograph is a modern day view - 2006 of the top postcard. Rehoboth Church still stands as a High Street landmark, while where Pendre Cottages once stood is today occupied by the shops Fresh 'n' Healthy, Morrice Evans Opticians, Musical Tools, Powell's the Jewellers and Bargain Booze.

Tales from the cinema

The top postcard looks down Rhyl High Street in 1921 from where Woolworths is today towards Vale Road bridge. The white-fronted building on the right (which is now McDonalds) was once known as Tottenham Buildings and housed the Picturedrome Cinema. It opened on May 22, 1911, but was commonly known as 'Kirks' after its owner Henry Kirk. It must be remembered that films were silent in those days with musical accompaniment from a piano or an organ. Admission to the Picturedrome cost threepence (1 1/2p), fourpence (2p), sixpence (2 1/2p) and one shilling (5p).

The first Charlie Chaplin films were shown at the Picturedrome with the music for the films played on a piano by a Mr Bowen who had a habit of disclosing the subsequent scenes of the film to the audience. In 1921 the Picturedrome changed owners and later became the Picture House Super Cinema (pictured) which introduced the serving of free cups of tea at matinee performances, before the sale of ice creams became commonplace.

The Picture House Super Cinema closed its doors to audiences for the last time on July 9, 1921. The first purpose-built cinema in Rhyl was the short-lived Cinema Royal. It opened in 1920 and was built on the site where Woolworths stands today. As a young boy, George Baker of Rhyl fondly remembers that the back door to the Royal was faulty and didn't completely close as it should.

So, following the departure of the cinema audience, George recalled he would sneak in through the back door and into the toilets where he would pick up a discarded sixpenny ticket off the floor and then make himself comfortable in one of the seats to await the next performance with a packed audience. George recollects that when Dolly Dyson the usherette came around to check the tickets, he would show her the half ticket he had picked up off the floor, with the usherette not knowing the difference in the dark.

He adds that there were two main features and a Mickey Mouse cartoon during the interval. The Royal closed in 1939. The bottom modern-day view of the 1921 postcard shows how McDonalds has replaced the Picture House Super Cinema and the Subway sandwich bar has replaced Stead and Simpsons and the shop to let next door (formerly Jasons). Pedestrianising this part of the High Street has given a clean and tidy image to Rhyl High Street, emblematic of the 1921 photograph - two thought-provoking views of Rhyl don't you think?

Gwespyr's Coast Road garage - a potted history

The photograph above vividly captures the spirit of the 1930s in this Gwespyr Coast Road petrol station and café scene (today's Lobitos garage) paying homage to the days when cars such as the Austin, Morris, Standard, Riley and Jowett dominated the roads and when the price of a gallon of petrol was one shilling and four pence (7p).

During the 1920s, Liverpool-born Robert Reed, who lived in Prestatyn, ran the garage here for many years up until he purchased land on Beach Road, Gronant which he developed into a campsite. He subsequently bought and ran his own shop and caravan site at Ty'n-y-Morfa, known as "Reed's Camp". Robert Reed eventually sold the garage in the 1930s and it came under the ownership of the Ellison's (pictured). Mr Ellison was a keen photographer who travelled around North Wales on his motorbike and sidecar taking photographs, besides taking photographs of customers who passed through his garage and café. Mrs Ellison who ran the café was noted for her high teas and her hospitality. During those alluring days of the 1930s as more people bought cars, the Ellison's garage and café was kept very busy from early morning until late at night, especially at the weekends. Seen in the doorway of the café is Miss Margaret Thomas who lived at Pant Glas Farm which is pictured in the background (the farm today is run by Leverett Contracting). Margaret Thomas worked at the café for many years until the beginning of Second World War when her work at the café was considered a non-essential occupation and she was required to work at the large Stork factory on the Wirral. After one year in the factory, Margaret Thomas moved back to Gronant where she was put in charge of a grocery store in the village for the remainder of the war. In 1958, when the price of a gallon of petrol was four shillings and seven pence (23 1/2p), the garage changed ownership and was bought by Muriel and Charles Smythe who had

moved from the Wirral to run the business. Muriel Smythe, today 90 years young, resides at Sandford Residential Home, Prestatyn. She told me that they renamed the premises, the Bungalow Garage and Ye Woodland Restaurant (pictured above in the 1960s), and recalls with the happiest of memories that her husband Charles ran the garage while she ran the popular upmarket restaurant.

Her husband Charles who has sadly since passed away, suggested at the time that they started selling chips to take out, which proved incredibly lucrative as queues appeared from the camp and caravan sites that populated Ty'n-y-Morfa, Gronant and Talacre in those days. They also ran a souvenir shop on the premises and worked from seven in the morning until two the following morning. Following many happy, hard-working and successful years at the Bungalow Garage and the Woodlands Restaurant on the Coast Road, Gwespyr, the Smythes retired in 1980. Muriel took up painting as a hobby - selling her work for a charity dear to her – the Leprosy Mission. Today Muriel has no shortage of company as she is surrounded by her children, Chris, Malcolm, Pauline and her nine grandchildren and six great-grandchildren who are all happy to listen to her illustrious reminiscences.

Muriel Smythe pictured today at 90 years young!

Happy days at Meliden

The village of Meliden with its strength of community still retains strong links with its history-steeped past, conspicuous by the distinctive stone-built miners' cottages in the village, evidence of a once-thriving and prosperous lead mining industry dating back to the 1840s (see page 10 of my book Memory Lane Volume I; pages 20 and 21, Memory Lane Volume II and pages 34, Memory Lane volume III).

The corner of Ffordd Talargoch and Ffordd Penrhwylfa, Meliden, is endearingly captured on this delightful postcard pictured above in 1930. The seven old cottages pictured, which were demolished in 1937, were known as Tai Cochion (red cottages) for the reason that they were built of red brick rather than the conventional limestone of the day. Today, the Red Lion car park stands here (the photo opposite is a present day view of where Tai Cochion once stood).

In his evocative recollections of old Meliden, Richard Jones of Isfryn Road, in the village, who has since sadly passed away, recalled during his youth that there were one or two noted characters in the village, one of them being Mr Roberts, the cobbler who lived at Tai Cochion and took in shoes and boots from people in the village for repair. The men of Meliden at one time visited Mr Roberts to air their views on the matters of the day, while he cobbled away. Richard recalled another remarkable character well-known in the village – a spinster with the nickname of Jane "Glastwr" (the welsh word for a mixture of milk and water). Not that she liked that sort of drink; she was partial to a stronger kind and would obtain her money by charring at the local farms. One trick she used, especially during the summer when there was a great number of visitors about, was to wrap her arm in bandages and stand somewhere conspicuous holding her bandaged arm across her chest. When she was approached, she

would inform them that she had been involved in a terrible accident and had a family to support. In sympathy, the gullible visitors would give her money. Sometimes Jane would try to sell turnips or cabbages which she said a farmer had given her lieu of payment.

Richard also recollected with the fondest of memories that, as a boy, he looked forward every Saturday to the greengrocers from Dyserth which stopped at intervals along Meliden's main street: *"Our delight was to purchase as much as possible for a penny (1/2p) we had to spend – probably two oranges or pears. Sometimes we would wait until the greengrocer's last call at the front of the Red Lion Inn and get a bargain in an assortment of leftovers and receive a bag-full for our penny."* I wonder what has become of those sweet and juicy small green pears we used to buy for a penny a pound. Richard recalled: *"They were called green chisels. Happy days when life was more contented, less pressurised and more reassuring."*

Pictured above in 1974 is Richard Jones (known as Richie) of Meliden, who has since passed away, left a valuable legacy in print of life in the village during his youth.

Treasured memories of the 'Fab Four'

A plea for help to the Beatles for a lift home by four Rhyl girls after seeing their performance at Prestatyn's Royal Lido in 1962 was met with such memorable witty remarks by John Lennon that the girls still remember them today with the valued memories they deserve. Best of friends to this day, Shirley Lloyd, Gill Evans, Jean Cummings and Mavis Dyson (pictured opposite) who all lived in Rhyl at the time, regularly spent their Saturday nights out together at the once very popular and prestigious Royal Lido Prestatyn (pictured above in the 1960s and later rebuilt as the Nova Centre in 1991).

Opened by the Duke of Gloucester in 1960, the Lido had a magnificent maple wood dance floor in front of a large stage (both still retained when the Nova was built) where the famous pop artists of the day appeared, including such greats as Billy Fury, The Searchers, The Tremeloes, Dave Berry, Billy J Kramer and The Dakotas, Lee Curtis and The All Stars, Screaming Lord Sutch and Geno Washington. The Beatles appeared at the Lido on November 24, 1962, for which they were paid £30 for their two-hour performance, having released their first record Love Me Do on October 5, 1962 (reaching number 17 in the charts). It was not until their first number one record Please Please Me in 1963 that "Beatle mania" gripped Britain and later the whole world. Alan Veech, the Lido's head chef recalls that The Beatles asked for a northern delicacy before going on stage: a plateful of jam sandwiches!

Having each paid six shillings admission (30p) to see the Beatles play at the Lido, the four Rhyl girls had missed the special laid-on bus from Prestatyn to Rhyl. Subsequently, they saw the Beatles and Cynthia Lennon loading up the van following their performance at the Lido (Cynthia and John were married on August 23, 1962). In desperation, one of the girls, Shirley Lloyd, shouted over to them "Any chance of a lift? We've missed the last bus home to Rhyl." As John and Paul walked over, Shirley shouted again *"Any chance of a lift home to Rhyl?"* to which John Lennon quips *"dems who misses the bus dems who die"*. Shirley responds by saying *"Thank you for being so sympathetic, the tears are streaming down your face."* To which John quips again *"Those are not tears they are warts."* Provoked by his reply.

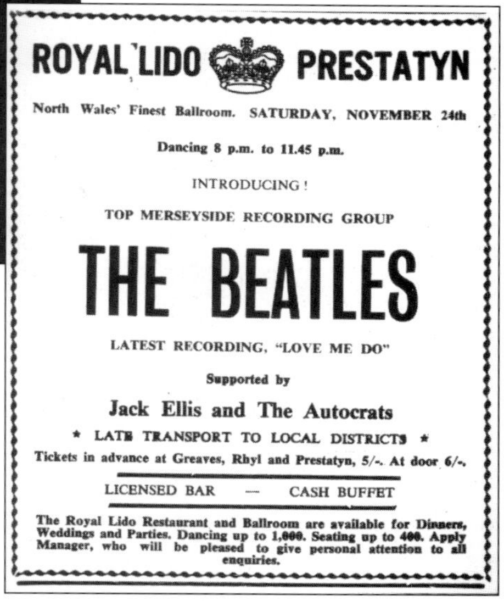

Shirley tells John *"I'm not going to buy your record now"*. John then informs Shirley with his usual comic flair *"That's OK I've bought five thousand copies myself."* Paul McCartney, standing next to John Lennon, asks Gill Evans *"Which one of you is Miss Rhyl?"* Gill recalls telling him *"The one with black hair."* Following their pleasurable exchange of witty remarks, John and Paul went back to loading the van, while the girls were left stranded until the Lido manager Fred Jackson, locking up the building , saw the girls and offered them their much needed lift home following a very memorable evening. Grateful thanks to Gill Evans of Rhyl for her precious memories and to my good friend Ray O'Brien of Liverpool for allowing me to quote from his latest book. *"There Are Places I'll remember; The Beatles around Merseyside and North Wales."*

Top left: Pictured left to right are: Joan Cummins, Shirley Lloyd, Gill Griffiths & Mavis Dyson c1960.
Top right: A poster advertising the gig.
Above: Fred Jackson, manager of the Royal Lido throughout the 1960s.

Link to the town's past

There can be no other town in North Wales that can speak more proudly of its cinema heritage than Rhyl. Here is a concise history.

The man responsible for the first screening of films to the public in Rhyl was cinematographer and entrepreneur Arthur Cheetham, who has bequeathed a rich archive of locally-shot film to Rhyl, leaving a valuable and important link to the town's past. Arthur Cheetham's earliest reference to screening films to the public, which were films he filmed himself, of local scenes and events, was at Rhyl's Town Hall in 1897 (see pages 20, 25, 59 of my book Memory Lane Volume III). This was a mere year following the world's first showing of "moving pictures" in Paris, by the Lumiere brothers in 1896. Arthur Cheetham subsequently opened Rhyl's first cinema, the Central Cinema at the Lyric Hall, Market Street, in 1906 and it was said to be the first cinema in Wales (the rooms are above today's Farmer's Market fruit and vegetable shop) also known as the "laugh and scratch".

These were the very early days of cinema, when going to the cinema to see the silent films of Charlie Chaplin, Buster Keaton, The Keystone Cops and Pearl White became a great adventure, with music to accompany the films being played on a piano by a Miss Peacock of Meliden. The Central later changed its name to the Silvograph, and in 1929 was acquired by Rhyl Entertainments Limited who owned the cinema Royal, (where Woolworth's is today, see page 18 of Memory Lane Volume II).

The Silvograph closed in 1931. Arthur Cheetham eventually went to Los Angeles to study film-making. He died in 1936. During subsequent years, cinema-goers in Rhyl had the choice of three principal cinemas- The Plaza, Odeon and Regal. The Plaza (pictured above in 1937) sited where the Piazza restaurant is today, was opened in 1931 boasting a seating capacity of 1,600 with admission prices of one shilling (5p) – one shilling and three pence (6 1/2p) – and one shilling and sixpence (8p). One of the first films screened at the Plaza was Charlie Chaplin's 1931 masterpiece City Lights, telling the

story of a tramp and a blind flower girl he falls in love with. At the time, Charlie Chaplin went against the incoming tide of *"talking pictures"* by using only music and sound effects and his own pantomime skills. It became a resounding success. In the 1960s, the Plaza was taken over by the Hutchinson Group, with seating on the ground floor being used for bingo and the cinema restricted to the balcony. The Plaza closed in 1986.

At the cost of £68,000 with seating for 1,400 the Odeon opened in 1937 with the Floral Robson and Leslie Banks film Farewell Again, which in those days also featured a Gaumont British News feature and a cartoon with the main film. The Saturday matinees at the Odeon became a great success as children hissed and booed the villains and cheered the heroes in the films of Flash Gordon, Roy Rogers, Hopalong Cassidy and Laurel and Hardy. In the late 1930s, the Odeon introduced the Mickey Mouse Club, with the club song words: *"Every Saturday morning where do we go, getting into trouble, oh dear no, to the Mickey Mouse Club with our badges on, every Saturday morning to the O-Dee-on"*, It changed ownership in 1969 and became the Astra, then a multi-screened cinema in 1972. The Old Odeon building is today in use by the Apollo Bingo.

The last purpose-built cinema in Rhyl, the Regal, opened in 1937, and was one of the very first cinemas to install cinemascope. One of the first films screened at the Regal was Broadway Melody, the 1937 film in which Judy Garland sang Dear Mr Gable (Clarke Gable), to the tune of "You made me love you". Admission prices to the Regal were one shilling (5p) – one shilling and nine pence (9 1/2p) – and sixpence (3p). The manager of the Regal, until its closure in 1962, was Leslie Spencer. The old Visitor newspaper offices and Lloyd's pharmacy today occupy the site where the Regal once stood. It is rather thought-provoking that Rhyl once had only one cinema, Arthur Cheetham's Central Cinema. Today one hundred years on, Rhyl continues to possess only one cinema, the Apollo.

Opposite page: The Plaza, High Street, Rhyl, pictured in 1937.
Above left: The Odeon, Brighton Road, Rhyl, pictured in 1948.
Above right: Photo of Mickey Mouse Club Badge.

Messages from the 'other side'

For most people, the word ghost conjures up a transparently hooded white figure that is likely to been seen in a stately home, mansion, castle, or old church, which couldn't be further from the truth. Ghosts and haunting sounds are in existence all round us, in our modern-day homes, buildings, shops, pubs and the roads we travel along.

Everyone knows someone who has seen a ghost, whether it was a figure dressed in Victorian clothes seen in a window, a room in a house or the ghostly sounds of children at play in the yard of a modern-day home that was built on the site of an old school. There is a strong indication that one person in 10 will see a ghost or experience some kind of ghostly encounter during their lifetime. This is one eerie experience from the tranquil village of Gronant. Mrs Henry Jones had lived a long, happy and respected life. She had built up a popular merchandise grocery business in the community spirited village of Gronant and married her second husband Henry Jones at the local chapel - Capel-y-Groes. But she lay dying in the bedroom of her home in Gronant where she and her husband Henry had lived happily for many years. The District Nurse was in attendance and Henry unable to stand the pain of the woman he had loved for all those contented years slowly departing from his life, went downstairs and sat himself in his favourite armchair waiting for the summer's evening to end and to reflect on their years together. His wife had been a bossy woman and was never ill up until now and he had got quite used to being ordered about by her. He now pondered who would look after him after she had gone. Feeling heartbroken, empty and alone, nothing could console him from what he saw was an inevitable catastrophe in his life. The grandfather clock at the foot of the stairs that had been in their home since their marriage struck the hour. Henry yawned and considered going to bed to lie down, but the thoughts of his wife deprived him of any sleep that night while she lay dying. He shook his head in bewilderment. Surely he thought the clock had struck midnight, but it was still striking. He sat up in astonishment and counted the strokes of the clock, seventy-three, seventy-four, seventy-five. Mercifully, it stopped as the nurse came through and told Henry his wife had peacefully passed away. Henry's wife was 75 and he firmly believed his wife's departed soul was at rest and peace the precise moment the clock had stopped striking 75. He also believes that to this day her message from the *"other side"* was clear. She would forever be looking over him at his home in Gronant where he still lives with his beloved grandfather clock.

The old cottages

At the end of Sandy Lane, Prestatyn can be seen traditional Welsh cottages built in Prestatyn's halcyon days before the opening of the Chester to Holyhead railway and when Prestatyn was a picturesque village with a scattering of thatched cottages and a population of 200. Over the years, Lavender Cottages (known today as Tai Tywyn) have undergone extensions and alterations by Rhuddlan Borough Council and today have been taken over by Denbighshire County Council as office space for small businesses.

The once simple two-roomed cottages: one room was the bedroom, the other a living area and kitchen combined – would have had an open fire or iron range for cooking and a large fireclay sink with timber draining boards. Water would have been brought from a nearby stream or a shared standpipe and tap. The walls and ceiling of the cottages were covered with lime plaster and painted, while the floors may have originally been of beaten earth covered with slate slabs or large quarry tiles, oil lamps and candles provided light.

The first owners of Lavender Cottage were Meliden lead miner Peter Jones and his wife Mary Hughes who built the cottage in 1840, and supplemented his income by working the acre or so of land around the cottage. In 1884, the cottage was bought by the Reverend John Townsend of Birmingham for £135 and in September 1900, it was sold again and purchased, this time by labourer William Parry for £230. He died in 1927, leaving the property to his wife Elizabeth. Elizabeth died six years later on February 9, 1933, leaving Lavender Cottage to her two children, Sarah and John. Sadly when they both died John in 1975 and Sarah in 1982.

The cottages were left open for sale until December 14, 1984 when they were purchased by Rhuddlan Borough Council. Many homes such as Lavender Cottages built in the 18th and 19th centuries have been long abandoned or developed to provide dwellings of modern standard. The preservation of well-built stone cottages is important if we are to understand the lives of their builders, inhabitants and their customs. The cottages in Sandy Lane, Prestatyn are just that – a superb and invaluable slice of history.

Above left: The cottages commonly known as Fisherman's Cottages, Glan-y-Gors, Sandy Lane pictured in 1991.
Above right: The same cottages pictured in 2006 some years after refurbishment.

Rhuddlan's old National School

Rhuddlan's heritage and history is unsurpassed in the district and there can be very few towns in Wales that can boast such a unique historical legacy (see pages 46, 47 of my book Memory Lane, Volume I). Rhuddlan is recorded in the Doomsday Book of 1086 as Roeland, the town's name changed frequently through the centuries from Rothelan, Rudlan, to Ruthlan. Its present spelling appeared around 1577 but was not officially used until 1896 when the local council gave the name its approval.

The postcard above is Rhuddlan's National School, Castle Street during the early 1900s. The school was built in 1829. When it closed in the early 1930s, a more modern and bigger school, Ysgol y Castell in Hylas Lane, was opened in 1935. In 2005, the school celebrated its 70th anniversary with a dance at the Faenol Fawr for ex-pupils and teachers. The old building was later to become a meeting place for the British Legion. Between 1979 and 1984, the National School Building went through extensive modernisation and is today the beautiful home of a local businessman, pictured above right in 2006.

Schooldays are supposedly the best days of your life but there are no smiling faces here (right photo) of Rhuddlan's National School pupils in 1904. The head master Bellis Jones of Holywell seen on the left. He earned £90 a year as head master and left in 1914 to receive a higher wage of £110 a year at a school in Dyserth. Mr Hugh Jones took over as the new head master at the National School. He left in 1922 and Mr Alec Jones became the head master. The large building on the right beyond the school is Tower House, in those days a newsagents and confectioners owned by two sisters, a notice in their window informed customers *"No papers sold on Sunday"*.

Today Tower House has been converted into a private tenement with opulent views of the castle. Opposite Tower House was Mr Williams Edwards and Sons butchers.

The best days of our life...

I wouldn't say that time flies the older we become, but it certainly doesn't crawl like it used to, does it? As the years pass and mellow, we marry, have children and see them through school, recollecting to them our own schooldays, said to be *"the best days of our life"* in which we all have memorable moments that we often reflect on. Bobby Walker of Prestatyn kindly loaned the above photograph for me to copy of Prestatyn's Clawdd Offa Secondary Modern School for my archives (today known as Prestatyn High School).

He recalls his memorable moments at the school when he was caught smoking behind the school gym and was called onto the stage during morning service the following day in front of the whole school to be "taught a lesson" by the headmaster Dan Owen who had hidden a cane behind the stage curtain. Bobby was given "six of the best" across his behind. And had he been taught a lesson following that chastisement? Of course he hadn't in that he was caught smoking again, this time by the headmaster himself who *"I think had given up on me"*, said Bobby, as he told me *"Walker if you want a cigarette, have one at home with your dad in front of the fire"*.

The photographs pictured here are a class of 2E who walked the corridors of Clawdd Offa in 1956. They are:
Top row L-R: Ted Jones, John Emlyn Jones, Robert Foulkes, Paul Hughes, Roy Griffiths, Cyril Taylor, John Hughes, Dave Roberts, Unknown, Gerald Davies.
Second row L-R: Anita Harris, Rozalin Parkinson, Unknown, Susan Williams, Norma Evans, Pat Franey, Mary Evans, Pamela Hennesey, Unknown, Unknown, Unknown,
Third row L-R: Barbara Jones, Unknown, Ann McMann, Janet Williams, Rita Jones, Unknown, Dora Jones, Margaret Fisk, Edna Jones, Unknown,
Front row L-R: Bobby Walker, Barnie Benbow, Idris Morris, Dennis Roberts. Can anyone fill in the unknown names for me?

The star of Rhyl

I have known the delightful Tracy Pimley of Rhyl since those heady and vibrant days of Rhyl's Palace disco during the 1970s and 80s and unexpectedly met her in Prestatyn in 2005 after not having seen her for two years. The first thing that captivates you about Tracy is her bubbly infectious personality and as we chatted about life, the universe and everything. Tracy told me that she had a reel of film from when she was Rhyl May Queen in 1970 and was it of any interest for my collection! Tracy had not seen the film since it was professionally filmed 36 years ago and I told her that a friend of mine Brian Mival had the means to transfer the film onto DVD. I eventually obtained the film and Brian subsequently digitally remastered it, adding titles and music to his finished production. I took the completed DVD to Tracy's and we watched the film as she narrated its content.

To say that Tracy was overjoyed with the DVD would be an understatement, with bursts of varying emotions. It starts with Tracy as a nine-year- old Rhyl May Queen, leaving her parents home in Princess Elizabeth Avenue, Rhyl, and into the car to the Ocean Beach where she took her Queen's seat on a float in a procession that was escorted with full pageantry along Wellington Road and onto the Pavilion Theatre for the May Day show.

The fascinatingly charming period film shows many long since gone Rhyl landmarks and close-up shots at the Pavilion of many familiar local faces, Tracy recognising many of her friends' parents. Tracy later informed me that the DVD is a fantastic piece of history that she will pass on to her grandchildren. I can see that it had a marked effect on her, as the film captures the spirit of the age. Following her May Queen title, Tracy also became Empress of Prestatyn carnival in 1970, and Rhyl Rounders Queen 1979.

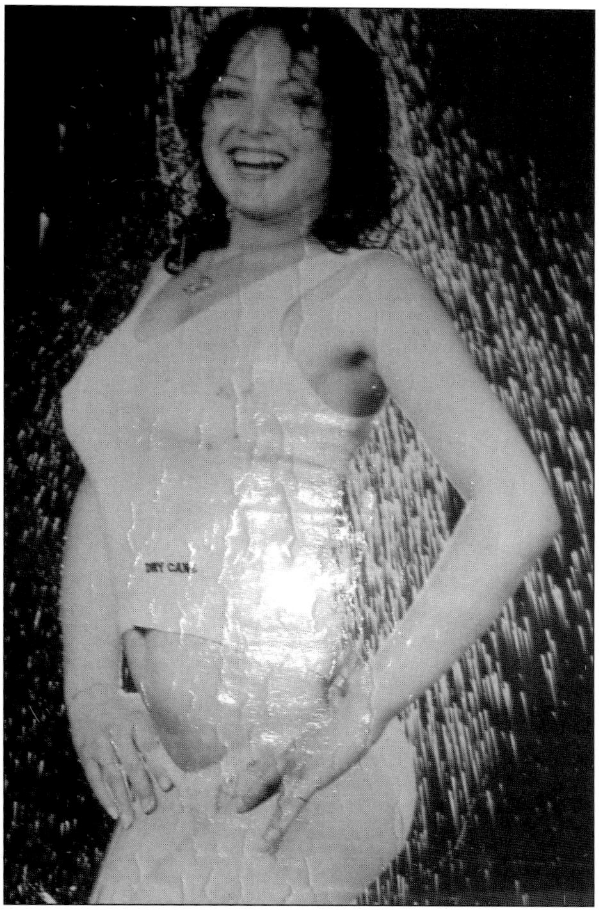

With Tracy's attractive looks and bubbly personality, it came as no surprise to me that Tracy won the very first Miss Wet T-shirt Contest at the once renowned Stables, Talardy, St Asaph, in 1979 when it was owned by entrepreneur Louis Parker of Rhyl. The publicity for the contest was enormous as was the audience. The 18 finalists in the new-style beauty contest were asked questions and winner Tracy was asked what her ambitions were, to which she replied *"to marry the Cat"*, the nickname for her boyfriend Alan. Tracy received £2,000 and bottles of spirits and glasses from the sponsors, and appeared in national newspapers. She also received lucrative offers from Playboy and Mayfair magazines but had to decline the offers due to her pregnancy. When a club boss in Bermuda picked up the Miss Wet T-shirt idea, the police chief poured water on it, proclaiming it would start a riot. And yes Tracy married Alan *"the cat"* in 1983, and they had three children. Tracy today is a proud grandmother of three grandchildren. Reflecting on the past and the future of fame and fortune and what she could have had. Tracy lit up with a smile and said *"I'm happier now than I have ever been"*.

Opposite page: Royalty: nine year old Tracy crowned 1970 Rhyl May Queen by Carnival Queen of Britain Joyce Taylor at Rhyl's skating rink.
Top left: Tracy looking stunning as she takes a shower for a publicity photograph that appeared in the national newspapers in 1979.
Top right: Tracy as she is today.
Bottom photo: Tracy being interviewed by Stables owner Louis Parker following her success at winning the Miss Wet T Shirt Contest.

Prestatyn's Cinema heritage

Prestatyn's once prestigious 1,000 seater Palladium Cinema building with combined upstairs café built by Prestatyn builders Roberts and Sloss opened on May 15, 1921, with the largest audience ever gathered in a building in Prestatyn at that time. One thousand people from Prestatyn and the neighbourhood filled the Palladium seats for an inaugural musical concert given by Prestatyn Choral Society, followed by a rendition of songs by renowned Prestatyn baritone Wilford Roberts, tenor Tom Jones of Gwespyr, and soprano Helen Jones of Caradoc Road, Prestatyn, who along with Wilford Roberts had won many Eisteddfod cups for their singing. Wilford Roberts ran a butchers shop in Prestatyn High Street and is still trading today under his grandson John Roberts, having recently received the Prestatyn and District Business Association's Best Small Business Award 2006 for the second year in succession. A large framed photo of John's grandfather can be seen in the butcher's shop window today.

The very first film shown at the Palladium in 1921, when films were silent, was Wolves of the Night, followed in later weeks by Winchester Women and The Shark, advertised as a thrilling sea story. During subsequent years, the Palladium drew vast audiences, and for the price of a cinema ticket in the 1920s of nine pence (four and a half pence), one shilling and three pence (six and a half pence), one shilling and ten pence (9p) or two shillings and four pence (22p), a uniformed usher led Cinema-goers up the marble stepped entrance, and on admission usherettes showed them to a carpeted cinema with tip-up upholstered seating (a luxury in the days when many cinemas were known as *"flea pits"* or the *"laugh and scratch"*)

Courting couples were shown to the balconies to *"courting couples"* seats (two seats in one). Eighty-five-year-old Fred Hobbs of Prestatyn recollects with his fondest of memories as a young boy in the late 1920s going to the Palladium with a gang of friends and paying three pence (one and a half pence) for the

front row seats to see the films of cowboy Tom Mix, Laurel and Hardy, the Keystone Cops, and Buster Keaton (all silent). Alfred Stagg of Maes-y-Groes, Prestatyn, was the pianist whose music accompanied the films. During the interval, Fred recalls that a tattooed man and his wife paraded among the cinema audience as entertainment. Throughout those early days of cinema along with the main feature films of Rudolph Valentino, Al Jolson, and Paul Robeson's Desert Song, there was also a Felix the Cat cartoon.

The 1920s also saw the sing-along at the Palladium. Words were displayed on the screen, and a bouncing ball would follow the words to the song as the audience sang accompanied by Alfred Stagg on the piano.

In the late 1940s, Archibald Stanring was Palladium doorman usher, and the usherettes were Helen Jones, Florence Harding, Megan Davies, Margaret Limburn, Joan Hayes, Eirwen Davies, and Micki Craven. The Palladium manager from 1932 until the late 1940s was Harold Monday.

The Palladium had a strong sense of belonging to Prestatyn and was demolished in 1978, long before it had attained a building of any age, yet it is a cinema that will be etched in people's memories for a long time. Boots the Chemist today stands on the old Palladium site.

1940's Palladium Cinema Staff.
Micki Craven, Joan Hayes, Florence Harding, Helen Jones, Megan Davies, Margaret Limburn, Eirwen Davies

Ghostly encounter at old cemetery

Rhyl's Holy Trinity Church in the grounds of St Thomas' Church, Russell Road, was built in 1835. No provisions were made for burials on the site, and many continued to take place in Rhuddlan. However on June 15, 1859, a small plot of land in Morley Road on the corner approaching Grange Road Bridge was consecrated by the Bishop of St Asaph to be the church cemetery for Rhyl. The first burial, that of a young girl, took place that afternoon. By the late 1880s, all available plots at Morley Road Cemetery had been taken, and a plot of land in Dyserth Road opposite the municipal cemetery was to be used as a church cemetery. The Bishop of St Asaph consecrated this new church cemetery on June 1, 1891.

No new graves were opened at Morley Road after 1891, but some burials continued in existing graves until the 1930s. The Morley Road cemetery was landscaped in 1967 and all monumental inscriptions were recorded and indexed and are today held at Rhyl library. During the time the headstones were still standing at Morley Road Cemetery, Chris of Rhyl vividly recalls the day he, as a ten-year-old, and his friends saw a figure of a young girl dressed in old fashioned clothes there. Chris and his friends were playing football on a hot summer's day on the road near the cemetery and were told by passing adults not to play on the road due to the traffic which resulted in the boys climbing over the Morley Road cemetery wall where they found a space large enough for them to continue their game without being disturbed – or so they thought. Near the space where they were playing football was a narrow path leading from the end of the cemetery and it was along this path that their ball landed and stopped near a little girl about two or three years old, dressed in old fashioned clothes. Chris' thoughts were more on his game of football than the distractions of a little girl and he asked her to kick the ball back to him. Chris vividly recalls that she wore a hat and coat over a frilled bottom dress, and that they were grey in colour. She didn't move and had her head bowed with her hands behind her back in a shy posture. Chris also recalls his friends who also saw her and were all shouting for her to kick the ball back to them. At that time, they thought that it was very strange and unusual that she should be wearing so much clothing on such a hot day, besides, they were old fashioned clothes. For a very good reason, one of the boys shouted *"she's a ghost"*, by which time they had all climbed back over the wall. When the momentary scare had subsided, their first thoughts were on retrieving their football and the boys together climbed back over the cemetery wall. They retrieved their football and the little girl in Victorian dress had disappeared as unexpectedly as she had appeared.

Chris recalls the day he and his friends encountered the ghost of the shy little Victorian girl as if it was yesterday and it has left him with a lasting impression he will never forget. His own conclusions are: *"some of those graves at Morley Road cemetery were very old perhaps the ghost of the little girl was drawn to us because of the noise and laughter of our play."* Or possibly Chris, the first interment at Morley cemetery was that of a young girl – was that her apparition?

Today, Morley Road cemetery is a pleasant open-space park, designed and planted with new landscaping, shrubs, sensory garden, seating, CCTV and lighting, which is fenced and gated and for the people to enjoy, opened on May 26th 2006.

Pocket history of Bodnant School

The prestigious Bodnant Infants School building in Marine Road, Prestatyn has changed very little in the past 100 years, surviving two world wars, unrest, and the designs of property developers. This is a brief history of the school. Originally known as the Board School, due to the fact that it was run by a board of the town's dignitaries, the school was built to replace the overcrowded and insanitary British School in Caradoc Road, built way back in 1891 and also that it had not come up to the requirements of the British Board of Education. Today, the old British School building is in use as a popular community centre known as Ty Caradoc. The land for building Bodnant School was bequeathed by Lady McLaren, the daughter of industrialist Henry Pochin, who developed Prestatyn into a clean and modern town. Built from Ruabon red brick at a cost of £1,425 and to accommodate 150 children in two large classrooms (today Bodnant has 300 children), the school was opened on October 17, 1902, by A G Leggard, his Majesty's Chief Inspector of Schools. By 1904, gardening had become part of the school's curriculum for those boys not academically minded. The school had its own plots situated at the front of the school. One plot was devoted to growing vegetables and the other for growing flowers. The gardening was under the guidance of headmaster Tom Roberts. The boys were later allowed to take the fruits of their work back home to their proud parents. People passing stopped to watch the boys and would marvel at their gardening skills. The only other school in Wales in those days with gardening on the curriculum was at Glyn Ceiriog. The girls at the school were taught domestics which included sewing, knitting, nature studies and cooking. During those early years, the children didn't wear uniforms and they wrote with pen, nib and ink; ink monitors filled the ink wells in the desks each morning from jugs and powdered ink. On winter mornings, there was an open fire in the classroom, and one child was chosen each morning to keep the fire going all day. When the school was inspected in 1905, the report read: "The children are clean and orderly and attend with commendable regularity. The cottage gardening has proved most successful and stimulates the boy's interest and their surroundings. Miss Lloyd's methods quicken the intelligence of the children who are happy, comfortable and well taught." There were no school meals until the canteen was built in 1945 and lunch was eaten in the classroom. The school's name was changed to Bodnant in 1961 and today still remains at the heart of the community, helping each child to reach their full potential while being individuals.

Top photo: Infants Board School 1926 – 1927

Bottom photo: Back row L-R, Cecil Jones, Freddy Roberts, Willie Parry, Peter Jones (Lived with his grandmother who made her own soap), Harry Parry, Fred Hobbs, John Owen, Tudor Morris, Emlyn Williams, Austin Bennett (Father captain of Prestatyn Fire Brigade),
Middle row L-R: Reggie Jones, Unknown, Betty Lawton, Mary Jones, Megan? , Myfanwy Williams, Betty Jones, Doris Williams, Margaret Hughes
Bottom row L-R: Unknown, Clem Ellis, Unknown, Nonie Sellers, Emrys Hughes, Unknown, Dilys Davies, Lawrence Williams, Jimmy Roberts, Miss Lawton (Teacher).

Scene from the past tells a story

One of the greatest pleasures of collecting old picture postcards of Prestatyn, Rhyl and the locality, is the discovery of superb social history postcards that tell a story.

As does the old postcard pictured here which was found in a box of old postcards marked *"Clwyd"* at one of the many postcard fairs held each month around the country that I frequently visit. The superlative scene shows firemen from Rhyl Fire Brigade as they attend to extinguish a fire at Rhuddlan in 1910, at a time when the fire engine was horse drawn and water to extinguish the fire was pumped from the engine by hand. The wonderful period picture postcard shows smoke still billowing from the fire in the houses as the firemen waste valuable time to pose for this photograph, in the days when having your photograph taken was more important than thoughts of the fire it seems, although to give the firemen the benefit of the doubt the fire was extinguished with no danger to the lives of the residents. The three houses were part of a row known as Highfield Terrace in Hylas Lane, Rhuddlan, and at the time occupied by a Mr Hodges, Mr and Mrs Lloyd Edwards and Mr Hatwood. The residents of the houses had gone to bed that Sunday night on November 20th, 1910. Around 2.30am, occupants of the middle house, Mr and Mrs Lloyd Edwards, awoke to find the room filled with smoke. On further inspection, the downstairs rooms were ablaze and the fire had spread to the houses either side. The occupants of these houses were awoken by the loud screams of Mrs Lloyd Edwards which lead to them running into the road outside. Conwy Bell, Captain of Bodrhyddan fire brigade was soon on the scene but when he saw the size of the fire, he had to contact Rhyl Police Station to call out the Rhyl Fire Brigade. In the meantime as Bodrhyddan Fire Brigade went to pump water on the fire, severe frost in the night had frozen the water and had stopped the hand pump from working to extinguish the fire. It was one and a half hours later at 4am before the Rhyl Fire Brigade arrived to extinguish the fire. The estimated amount of damage was £100, a huge amount in 1910.

The second photograph is Highfield Terrace as it looks today.

Romantic days of holiday season

Throughout the holiday season at Rhyl in the early 19th and 20th century, crowded steam packet boats the St Elian, Benledi and the Snowdon, ferried vast numbers of passengers from the Foryd Harbour and Rhyl's pier jetty to Liverpool for a return fare of three shillings (15p) and occasionally to Llandudno, Bangor and Beaumaris. Affording visitors, day –trippers and locals an opportunity of seeing the North Wales Coast's beautiful scenery.

At East Parade, Rhyl, near the Sun Centre, an historic 200 year old building can be seen that today stands as an illustrious monument that harks to those romantic and graceful days when steam-packet boats plied the North Wales Coast. Pen-y-Don (above the wave) Tower was built by John Tarlton in the early 19th century, who in 1895 lived in East Parade and was receiver of the Admiralty, and built the Tower as a semaphore signalling station for steam-packet boats operating between the Foryd Harbour and Liverpool.

Prior to the invention of the Telegraph, one method of signalling shipping was by means of flags from high towers such as Rhyl's Pen-y Don Tower which was used to transmit messages between distant points. Messages were read through a high powered telescope and were accomplished by a semaphore signaller in the tower who had a small flag in each hand and with arms extended moved them to different angles to indicate the letters of the alphabet or numbers. Pen-y-Don Tower was listed as of special historical interest as a grade two listed building in 1988 by the Secretary of State for Wales. It was restored to its former glory by David McLean's Construction in 1991.

Behind Pen-y-Don Tower was the once prestigious Pen-y-Don Tea House where Whitchurch born composer Edward German (1862 – 1936) stayed while visiting Rhyl and where he conceived the famous operetta Merrie England in 1902. While in Rhyl he also took time to visit his uncle - Rhyl photographer Ernest Jones who lived in Beachwood Road. Edward German was the first composer to write music for a British film which accompanied a scene for the film King Henry VIII. Pen-y-Don Tea House was demolished in the 1960s and Bradshaw Manor Nursing Home was built on the site in 1992.

Top photo: The St Elian Steam Packet boat packed with passengers as it leaves the Foryd Harbour for Liverpool in 1919.
Middle photo: Pen-y-Don Tea House, East Parade in the 1940s.
Bottom photo: Pen-y-Don Tower as it looks today.

The day the post went up in smoke

The post office is an old institution, and also one of the best known national institutions which directly affects people's daily lives. This is a potted history of Prestatyn's post offices. The first known post office in Prestatyn was in use in the middle 1800s from premises known as London House on the corner of Meliden Road and Plas Uchaf Avenue in the days when purchasing stamps and sending telegrams were the principal transactions. Today, Pen-y-Cae Homes for the elderly are situated where this post office once stood. In the late 1800s Prestatyn's post office was located at the top of High Street in Bradford Buildings, opposite Rehoboth Church. The postmaster was Griffith Eames. In later years, the post office operated from the corner of the High Street and Nant Hall Road (today's Card Warehouse), built in 1894 with part of the building set aside as a grocers, D J Price, son of the man who built the building, was appointed postmaster. However, one Sunday afternoon in 1899, the postmaster had retired upstairs for a nap, when Jonah Jones living opposite noticed smoke coming out of the post office and ran across the road and sounded the alarm by pulling on the post office's entrance bell, which awoke the postmaster who, on seeing the fire, telephoned Rhyl Fire Brigade. Prestatyn was without a fire service until 1900 and was formed due to a call for a fire service after this post office fire. The postmaster's first concern was the contents of the post office, but he was overpowered by the smoke and flames and made hasty retreat into the street. Next-door to the post office was EH Parry's ironmongers where a large quantity of explosives and gunpowder were kept in stock, but with admirable coolness, estate agent Frank Jewell entered the shop and carried it all to safety, which, otherwise would have resulted in half the street being blown up. It took one and a half hours for the horse-drawn fire brigade to arrive from Rhyl, as almost all the horses had been requisitioned

for summer visitors for pleasure purposes and only a horse and a small pony were found to pull the engine. It resulted in the total destruction of the building, with an estimated damage of £4,000. At one time, there was a post office located in the middle of the High Street opposite the church gates (where the Beauty Spot salon is today). In its day the mail to this post office was brought on foot from Rhyl and boasted that *"the telegraph and also the telephone had been installed for the use of the public"*. In 1925, a sorely-needed new post office was eventually built in King's Avenue by Prestatyn builder W D Prescott at a cost of £2,800 in the days when a first class stamp was one old penny (half pence). In September 1915, a halfpenny war tax was added to the postage. Following 90 years of providing a postal service to generations of Prestatyn people, the King's Avenue post office was closed in May 2006 and relocated at the bottom of the High Street inside the Spar shop after a £350,000 re-vamp. Will this new post office be given the stamp of approval for future generations of Prestatyn residents?

Opposite page: Prestatyn's Post Office on the corner of Nant Hall Road and High Street (today the Card Warehouse) with Rhyl Fire Brigade in attendance. The post office was totally destroyed in the the fire as this rare 1899 photograph shows.
Top photo: The old post office in the middle of High Street, opposite the Church gates pictured in 1912.
Bottom: The King's Avenue post office was closed in May 2006. My daughter Emma is pictured in the doorway the day before it closed.

Life on the buses among the rabbits on the Warren

Mention the renowned Warren that once graced Talacre to anyone who lived there and they will tell you of a happy and endearing community noted for its colourful characters. These folk lived for a time a graceful way of life in old caravans, wooden huts, mahogany panelled old double decker buses and old railway carriages of every description. The Warren ran along the sand dunes between Shore Road, Gronant and Talacre, taking its name from the huge rabbit population released to provide sport for shooters on the Talacre Hall Estates and supplement the food supply of its workers.

In 1920 the Warren was offered for sale with the rest of the estate, a sale made necessary due to crippling death duties. Subsequently a large number of extraordinary constructions appeared on the Warren and throughout the summer little shops and a bakery flourished (a favourite no doubt was rabbit pie!) while water was obtained in buckets from the trickling standpipes. June Tynan who has lived in Talacre for 50 years ran with her husband Jack the bakery on the Warren from 1956 until 1967 and frequently attracted lengthy queues for their deliciously home-made pasties, bread and cakes, and pays homage to the larger than life characters who lived on the Warren and Talacre. One colourful character was Les Hardcastle an eccentric ex-railway guard who shunned authority and who had the numbers 999 screwed to his gate and whose ramshackle dwelling was crammed to overflowing with wartime and railway memorabilia. Les became a regular site around Talacre, riding his bike with his pet parrot Polly towing behind in her cage. He later moved to Gamfa Wen opposite the old post office and during the summer kept Polly behind the hedge in his garden where she would mimic his neighbour, Vera Dulson's laugh which baffled passing holidaymakers. June recollects that Vera was another of Talacre's most colourful characters who lived opposite Les and had the ability to literally charm the birds from the trees which she fed in her garden. The birds would respond to Vera's whistling, and magically descend to be fed – a real life Mary Poppins in Talacre!

June also recalls Arthur and Joan Clewes who lived in an old bus on the Warren. Downstairs was their lounge and upstairs their bedroom and people came from all around to see it. When they moved to Gronant the bus was topped up with petrol, oil and water and driven to a museum in Liverpool.

For many years up until the late 1950s and 60s Percy Rice ran a General Store in Talacre and sold everything from nails to paraffin, cigarettes and fruit and veg. June recollects that a customer visiting the shop one day saw the lettuce move only to find that Percy's pet rabbit was among the vegetables nibbling away. Percy frequently served paraffin with the same unwashed hands that he would cut a piece of cheese for the customers. At night Percy used his talents at the piano to good effect at Talacre's Cardwell's Social Club. The boys of the Warren earned their pocket money visiting Point of Ayr Colliery's spoil heaps with their bikes and empty sacks which they then filled with coal and sold on to residents. At night however, they returned to pinch the coal which they had sold and returned a day or so later, selling it onto the same unsuspecting people. In the late 1960s the inhabitants of the Warren were offered Council Houses in Gronant and the last colourful character to leave the Warren who had geese and a goat in her garden as a "guard dogs" was 80 year old Lotti White who moved into a bungalow in Gronant.

Subsequently Presthaven purchased the Gronant end of the Warren for a Caravan Park, while the BHP Gas Terminal now occupies the Talacre end of the Warren which today has been transformed into a conservation area and a pleasant and popular walkway. The Warren had a great sense of belonging down Talacre and will be forever etched in the memories of those who remember it and a lasting testimony to the larger than life characters who lived there.

Opposite page: The Warren pictured in 1939
Above: June & Jack Tynan who ran a bakery on the Warren from 1956 to 1967, pictured here in 1959.

Ghostly sighting remains a mystery

On a warm and pleasant sunny summer's afternoon in 1986, eighteen-year-old Sheena Young and her father Richard, from Gronant, went for a drive through the tranquil and slumbering village of Llanasa. Heading out of the village along Llanasa Road towards Gwaenysgor, nearing a bend opposite Golden Grove and Home Farm, there is a picturesque leafy narrow lane, known as Lôn Ffynnon Llygoden (Mouse Well Lane). It was along this lane that Sheena and her father had a ghostly encounter that was so vivid that Sheena recalls her experience here in her own words.

"On approaching the bend in Llanasa which leads to a narrow lane opposite Golden Grove, my father commented that he had just seen what appeared to be a dray wagon. As he saw the driver perched high above the hedgerow, he wanted to stop to take a look at it, as he told me that he hadn't seen something like this for many years. As we neared the lane, we slowed down and approached cautiously and the dray became clearly visible, It was a fabulous sight – the old dray was painted in red and green and laden with wooden barrels being pulled by a magnificent shire horse adorned with fancy brass fittings either side of its bit and harness. The driver of the dray, a man of medium build and in his 50s, wore a huge brown leather apron and held a large whip in his hand along with the reigns. We both took in this wonderful sight and we very slowly passed the lane it was coming down and brought the car to a halt on the other side of the road, waiting momentarily for the dray to appear at the junction of the road. We waited but the dray did not make an appearance. We got out of the car and walked the few feet back to the junction where we expected to have seen the dray appear; and stood confused and bewildered as it was nowhere to be seen. As it was a very narrow lane and given the gradient of it, there seemed no possibility that the horse-drawn dray could have reversed back up the lane and also there was no possibility for it to have turned into a field as there were no gates or entrances of any kind, and the hedges were lush with growth, and the dray could not have passed us without us having seen it.

My father, after taking the logical view and finding no explanation for its disappearance, concluded that the only plausible answer was that we may have witnessed a ghostly encounter. The fact that remains in my memory of this 'sighting' was the feeling of reality I felt as if I could have actually physically touched the dray, perhaps even to the point of having made a polite, good afternoon gesture to the driver."

Today Sheena heads the prestigious UK Paranormal Investigation Team which she founded and is kept busy with historical researches and private investigations, and the group meets each month at Caskey's Pub, Vale Road, Rhyl. Sheena told me that her theory of the sighting at Llanasa was possibly a residual haunting, which is energy of a past emotion or event that is a playback known as the *"stone wall"* effect, where past events are recorded and played back possibly caused by determinant, atmospheric pressures, temperature and sidereal time. This is just one possible theory, the cause of residual haunting still remains a mystery.

Sheena Young at the Llanasa lane where, along with her father saw the horse drawn drey.

Fashionable days of Rhyl

Two contrasting thought-provoking views of the same part of Rhyl High Street showing the past and present looked at within 96 years of each other are showing the changes that have taken place within those years. The top photograph seen here for the first time depicts halcyon days in a cathedral-like quietness and a graceful way of life looking up Rhyl High Street in 1910 towards the promenade from the corner of Sussex Street (where the Piazza Restaurant is today). The boy on the left, wearing *"plus fours"*, a fashionable trouser of the day which derived their name from the fact that they fell four inches below the knee, adds charm to this delightful window into the past, along with the dog lying on the road. In all probability, this photograph was taken on an early Sunday morning, as in 1910, Rhyl was in the height of its popularity as a fashionable seaside holiday resort, attracting thousands from the industrial towns and cities of the North and Midlands to which the sea, sand, the pier, the Queen's Palace, Marine Lake Boating Park, Pavilion Theatre and the beach Pierrots, were the attractions of the day. The large building on the right was later developed and opened in 1920 as Rhyl's first purpose built cinema, the Cinema Royal, which closed in 1939 (see page 18 of my book Memory Lane Volume II). Woolworths which opened in 1954 stands there today. The little shops and businesses on the right comprised: a cycle depot, John Williams Portland Studios and X Ray Depot, Fredrick Heba Homan Barber and Tobacconist, Mrs Ingham Art, Needlework, Wool and Fancy Repository and J Mellard tobacconist. The drinking fountain in the distance on the promenade was erected in 1862 to commemorate the coming of age of Conwy Rowley Conwy of Bodrhyddan Hall located between Dyserth and Rhuddlan, who was Lord Langford's grandfather. The drinking fountain was later removed and today stands in the grounds of Lord Langford's Bodrhyddan Hall. The clock tower was built where the drinking fountain once stood in 1948. The bottom photograph is a modern day view (July 2006) looking up Rhyl High Street from the Piazza Restaurant. The shops on the right include Oggy Oggy Bakery and Coffee Shop, Bon Marche Ladies Outfitters, Shoe Express and Dolland & Aitchison.

Characters who left their mark

In every town and village, there are those residents who through their funny remarks, mannerisms or occupation became known as "local characters". Colourful, friendly and often eccentric, they were looked upon with great affection within their community. Invariably, they had nicknames suited to their own reputation such as Will Williams who was familiarly known as "*Wil-y-Bara*" (Will the bread). So named because he sold and delivered groceries and bread from the van of Gwespyr grocer A E Jones throughout Gwespyr and the neighbourhood in the 1950s and 60s.

Will, who always had a readily and friendly conservation with all his customers, was noted for his rapid conversations while he had a Woodbine cigarette permanently hanging from the corner of his mouth, and his eye blinking non-stop from the cigarette smoke.Will spoke so quick that you would be left standing wondering what his first words were while he was ending his conversation with you. Will married Sally in 1936 when he was a delivery boy delivering groceries down Talacre for one pound and one shilling (£1.05) a week, and they lived in Gwespyr for many happy years together. Sadly, "Will-y-Bara" died of a stroke in 1980 and is still fondly remembered today as one of nature's most loveable characters.

Another well-known, fondly remembered, colourful local character was Arthur Thomas, better known as "*Arthur Ice Cream*", a remarkable and enterprising individual who made his own ice cream to a special recipe at his home "Highlands" in Gwespyr. Arthur became a very popular and welcome sight during those long hot summers in the 1950s and 60s selling ice cream from his uniquely converted motorbike and sidecar in the villages of Gwespyr, Gronant, Ffynnongroyw, Penyffordd, Talacre, Trelogan, Mostyn and Bagillt. It was without any shred of a doubt the best ice cream in North Wales. One of my fondest lasting memories as a child was when my mother sent me with sixpence (3p) and a bowl to fill with ice cream when Arthur called. It was the same

bowl my mother put on our heads to cut our hair and by the time I had reached the door I had scooped half of the ice cream with my finger and had eaten it - delicious!

Ice cream cornets were tuppence (1p) and wafers one penny (1/2p) and tuppence (1p) or Arthur filled a bowl for sixpence (3p). Arthur retired in 1964 and sadly passed away in 2003. Arthur Thomas and his unrivalled ice-cream will, for many of us, linger long in the memory and our taste buds.

In every town and village there are those individuals who through their mannerisms became known as local characters - then there's John Bickley, pictured above right, of Llwyn Farm, Tan Lan, who can only be described as a living icon. John found celebrity status with his endearing gentlemanly manner on his milk round in Ffynnongroyw and the neighbourhood which he ran from 1930 up until 1980. His most noted customer was "*Arthur Ice Cream*" in the days when milk was tuppence (1p) a pint, butter one and three pence (6 1/2p) a pound, and cheese ten pence (5p) a pound, all home-made on the farm.

John was also well-known as a popular lay preacher for over fifty years packing many local churches with his entertaining sermons. John retired from the milk business in 1980 when a motorist ran into him while he was lifting a crate from his van, resulting in the loss of his right leg. At the age 84, John, with help, is still running his farm of cattle and sheep, which is one of the greatest pleasures of his life. He is also president of the coffee AM meetings along with Fred Hobbs and Betty Peters at Ty Pendre (next to the Cross Foxes pub) open each Thursday from 10am-noon for coffee, biscuits and a chat, all are welcome. Many of you will recall John's words when asked how he was, which were: "*busy, happy and well.*" Local characters that have left us and will leave us with an endearing indelible mark in the pages of our local history books.

Opposite page: Arthur Ice Cream obliging a Mrs Butterfield at Ffynnongroew with one of his deliciously home-made ices in the 1950s.
Above left: One of nature's most lovable characters "Wil y Bara" pictured here in the 1970s.
Above right: With a smile as big as his character, John Bickley was happy to pose for this photo I took of him in Prestatyn's Pendre Gardens in August 2006.

Hundred years of Prestatyn

Considering that the two photos pictured here of Prestatyn's High Street past and present were taken one hundred years apart, it is pleasantly surprising to notice minimal change, don't you think? The postcard above is an evocative view looking up the High Street in 1906, from where Ethel Austin is today, a superbly captivating scene capturing a strong sense of time, all but forgotten when life tiptoed by. A postcard that reflects a passion and a yearning for the past.

The oak trees behind the stone wall on the right is where the venerable Penisardre Farm once stood. During the reformation in the 16th century when monks and priests were being persecuted for their beliefs by government officials, they hid from their captors at Prestatyn in a "priest's hole" behind Penisardre's kitchen fireplace; and it was at Penisardre that Oliver Cromwell once stayed. In later years, Corbett Ellis lived at Penisardre running a prestigious business from the farm selling milk, cream, butter and eggs, and delivering his goods to customers twice daily by horse and cart. Up until the 1930s, Penisardre was still herding cattle twice daily to and from the fields and through the busiest part of High Street, much to the annoyance of the day's horse-drawn vehicles. Although visitors watched for hours and relished the rural activities of the farm – especially the piglets who seemed to habitually escape into the High Street. A Prestatyn woman passing Penisardre on her way to church one evening was surprised to be confronted by a large female sow. Mrs Corbett Ellis out looking for it said *"I wouldn't go near if I were you, she bites"*, I think the sow got the message!

Penisardre was demolished in 1964. Today, the shopping precinct stands on the former site, while the shops and business where the stone wall and oak trees once stood include Cumberlidge the jewellers, Bugatti Ladies Wear, Rumours Café, Serve-U-Rite Delicatessen, Contessa Ladies Wear, Abbey and Alec

Edward's shoe shop. The alluring building on the left built in 1897 today houses the HSBC Bank. The Town Hall next door was opened in 1900 by Lady McLaren. The planners had called it "*Manor Hall*" and it was built from Prestatyn brick, Ruabon brick and Gwespyr stone.

Prestatyn brickworks 1896-1920s was sited near Penrhwylfa crossroads on land where the Kingdom Hall of Jehovah church is today. In 1910, cinematographer "*Saronie*" who lived at Hill Court, Mount Ida Road, was showing films at the "*Town Hall*" advertised as an "*Exhibition of Animated Pictures*", By 1913, Saronie took over the Town Hall semi-permanently, later opening it as the first cinema in Wales, naming it La Scala (see page 44 of my book Memory Lane Volume I).

Sadly the Scala closed in 1999 accompanying an end to Prestatyn's romantic attachment to a much-loved and well-attended cinema, closing the curtains on an important part of the town's heritage and history and also an invaluable asset to Prestatyn's future.

The picture above is a modern-day view (July 2006) of the 1906 postcard opposite which shows that once tranquil way of life has today been lost by our love affair with the motor car. My son Harry was more than happy to be included in this present day photograph.

Sheep grazed on the wicket

Memory Lane reader Ena Allport of Meliden sends a copy of the column every week to her brother Philip Smith in Brighton, who at one time lived in Prestatyn's Dawson Park, which prompted him to send me an engaging lengthy letter and the photographs pictured. He recalled that he and some of his friends were "*very keen on cricket*" and that "*during the war we played on Bastion Ground of Prestatyn Cricket Club which in those days was derelict and used for sheep grazing*". Philip recollects: "*When we went to Rhyl's Grange Road County School (which subsequently became Rhyl Grammar School), some of us made it to the school's cricket first eleven in 1945.*

"The school liked its pupils to accept responsibility and before I become captain I had to spend a year as team secretary which meant having to arrange all the team fixtures against grammar schools at Holywell, Denbigh, St Asaph, Colwyn Bay and Abergele. As telephones were few and far between fixtures were arranged by post and I remember being told off by the Director of Education for failing to account for a penny stamp. "When I became captain in 1947, I had to organise the cutting of the pitch and its marking and rolling, and also the ordering of supplies of teas and helpers to serve. These were usually girls who were very keen on the boy cricketers. We were once out for nine runs against Colwyn Bay, and the highest score by a batsman was 32 runs by the late John Gilbert of Prestatyn. Our faithful scorer was Ivor Edwards who came to every match and it is thanks to him I have all the details in a notebook from the glorious summer of 1947".

Philip Smith's mother Annie Smith was widely known in Prestatyn during the 1940s for her well known smiling face who worked at the Old Kings Avenue Post Office.

Above: This photo is of Rhyl Grammar School Form Remove "A", July 1945.
Back row L-R: W Green, D Williams, B Dean, R W Jones, Sowcroft, D Manley, W Houghton, J Spencer, J Braka, J Windler, D R Hughes, J Grylls, K Eadie, R Harris, H Hodgood.
Middle row L-R: J S Weber Frimston, D McPhie, P C C Smith, W Wardle (form captain) A A Riley, J R Hicks, G Jackson, N Williams, P Wycherley.
Front row L-R: M Beardmore, H Adams, G Hughes, I Roberts, D Jones, H Sylvan Evans (form master) L Lilley, B Francis, J Roberts, M Hughes, D Donald, B Jones,

The photo above is Rhyl Grammar School First Eleven Cricket Team 1945.
Back row standing L-R: Osborne Owen (PT Master) Alan Riley, Ron Hicks, Jim Scowcroft, Derek Longrigg, Bob Jones, Philip Smith, Alan Vickery, Brian Dean (scorer).
Front row sitting L-R: John Weber, Michael Smith, Bill Wardle (captain). Derek Young, Colin Espley.
My grateful thanks to Philip for the photos and his absorbing reminiscences.

Bygone days of seaside shows

Picture this bygone scene and imagine yourself living in a noisy fume-filled industrial town or city in the North or Midlands. Picture those post depression days of the late 1930s, waiting to free yourself from the constant monotony and arduous toil of factory work for a seaside summer holiday on an excursion train – for those who could afford them – and to breath the invigorating health giving - ozone filled - bracing sea air. Tread the lengthy sands and enjoy the exhilarating entertainment of Prestatyn's Prestos, at the prestigious seaside resort of Prestatyn, in the days when the seaside holiday was a must for everyone. Those were the times, when you would take home with you valuable and unforgettable memories from a more glamourous and ageless era, distinguished by the innocent, clean family fun of Prestatyn's Prestos. Halcyon days when seaside shows were an established form of entertainment, and as much a part of a seaside holiday as the seaside comic postcard. Prestatyn's Prestos stage was sited near to where the amusement centre is today, near the Nova, where they entertained large audiences of visitors and locals with their gift of uplifting happy songs.

Dorothy Chard of Prestatyn affectionately recollects as a ten-year-old in 1934, that along with her sister Elsie while living in Sandy Lane, their mother promising them that they could go to the beach providing they called at Skelton Dowells Grocers (today's Spar on the corner of Victoria Park Avenue Road) and asked assistant Miss Griffiths to see them across the road. At a time when one car was seen to pass every five minutes. Walking down Bastion Road to the beach, Dorothy recalls the pony and traps overflowing with passengers going to and from the beach for a fee of a penny (1/2 p). Following their play on the beach, Dorothy and her sister would spend an afternoon watching the Prestos (pictured above in 1935) whose entertainment, accompanied by piano and drums, comprised of singing, comedy sketches, tap dancing, competitions and audience participation. Wooden railings encircled the front of the stage where the audience sat and stood and paid

sixpence (3p) to sit on deck chairs while those standing at the back paid three pence (1½p). Dorothy recalls the Prestos shows were always packed, and the happy songs she vividly remembers gave us both a laugh as she recalled some of their titles: *Lucy's Lipstick; How can a guinea pig show he's pleased if he hasn't a tail to wag; Let's have a tiddly at the milk bar; It's a party, gay and hearty; Let's have a jolly good game of darts; If only we had some eggs; The sun has got its hat on;* and *Smile when you wake up in the morning.*

In her endearing memories, Dorothy tells me about the day when Elsie and herself went up on the Presto stage to sing in one of their singing competitions, but her nerves got the better of her and she broke down in tears. Elsie, her sister, ended up singing on her own, but Dorothy received the prize of sixpence (3p), to her sister's displeasure. Dorothy and Elsie once entered their baby brother Malcolm in one of Prestos bonny baby competitions. He won and they received a voucher to spend at Goddard's Bazaar gift shop, next to the old Palladium Cinema (today's Boots the chemist). They obtained a spoon and pusher with their voucher. *"Needless to say, our mother was very cross with us for taking the baby onto the stage"*, Dorothy recalls. Endearing memories of halcyon days and a lament to the glamour and happy days of the seaside shows...

Opposite page: The comic of the troupe was Jimmy Oliver, seen here wearing the striped jacket. His wife Mollie is the woman in front of him.
Above: The Prestos stage pictured in 1933.
Below: Jimmy Oliver and Alf Howden pictured in Lower High Street, Prestatyn during the town's Carnival in the 1950s. Presto's Comedian Jimmy Oliver was an Illustrious attraction in each Carnival seen walking on stilts, he held a small pole with a bag on the end in which he collected money from the Carnival crowds. Alf Howden owned the White Rose Amusements sited on the corner of Bastion Road and Victoria Road. White Rose Close was built where the amusements once stood.

Stories of less hurried days

This postcard looking down Rhyl High Street with the children on the donkeys is an enchanting study of an elegant Edwardian summer scene in 1905. An illustrated guide to Rhyl of the day declared: *"Besides all the amusement. We must of course mention the children's delight to dig and romp on the sands; this is in fact an ideal place for children where plenty of perambulators and bath chairs are available as well as an unusual number of ponies and donkeys for hire."* The boarding house on the left later became the Cinema Royal, 1920 to 1939 (see page 18 of my book Memory Lane Volume II). Woolworth's built in 1953, stands here today.

Henkel's the ornate Victorian building on the right, was built in 1899, and sold beach accessories – note the wooden spades hanging outside. The Bright Spot amusements and Erbrium fashion accessories occupy here today. Henkel's had another shop on the corner of High Street and Russell Road (today Listers house furnishers) which sold fancy goods and toys and was advertised as *"The largest toy shop in Rhyl and cheapest house in town for presents, with a splendid stock of footballs, bladders, hockey sticks, table games, stuffed plush toys, and beautiful dolls a speciality."* This illustrious Rhyl shop had international customers who supplied their dolls to the Royal Houses of Europe (see page 14 of Memory Lane Volume II).

The postcard of Rhyl High Street from Vale Road Bridge which opened in 1855 is seen on the opposite page during the 1920s. Compared to a traffic congested road into the town today, we highly value old picture postcards that chronicle views such as this; a once tranquil and unhurried part of the town. The building on the left is the Alexandra Hotel, today Bar Blu stands here, while the building opposite is William Roberts's coal, corn, seed and hay and straw merchant, established in 1855. It later became a garden centre and shop for pet supplies (see page 46 of Memory Lane Volume III). William Robert's prestigious shop closed in 2005 when Robert Scott, the great grandson of the firm's

founder, took a well-earned retirement. At one time, the Villiers Hotel occupied the premises above William Robert's. Today, the extensive gift shop known as Shipley Street stands here (the old name for Brighton Road).

At the end of the terraced buildings on the right, the Odeon Cinema was later built and opened in 1937, where the very popular Saturday morning children's matinee became an uproar in the days when the children cheered the hero and hissed and booed the villain to such films such as Flash Gordon and the cowboy and Indian films of Roy Rogers and the Lone Ranger. The Odeon also introduced the Mickey Mouse Club in the 1930s and these were the words of their club song; *"Every Saturday morning, where do we go, getting into trouble, oh dear no, to the Mickey Mouse Club with our badges on, every Saturday morning, to the O-Dee-On."*

In 1969, the Odeon changed ownership and became the Astra. Today, the old Odeon building is occupied by Apollo Bingo. Which goes without saying that every picture postcard undeniably tells a story, don't you think?

Reminders of romantic past

The picture above of the middle of High Street, Prestatyn, ideally captures a strong sense of the period in this 1936 scene. Jones the outfitters on the left on the corner of Kings Avenue opened in 1914 as a milliners and gents outfitter owned by George and Edith Jones. George ran the gents department while his wife Edith ran the milliners department of the shop. Today Signature menswear occupies this building.

A 1936 holiday guide to Prestatyn declared within its pages: *"Above the main roads from east to west in Pendre is a spacious square wherein once the villagers lingered and gossiped and where curiously enough residents and visitors of the day love to sit in the sun and watch the briskly moving scene. Below the square is the High Street where most of the whitewashed and thatched cottages of fifty years ago have given way to up-to-date shops, banks, cafes, cinemas and other buildings, but there are plenty of reminders of a romantic past and it requires no effort of the imagination to conjure up a world of quaint yesterdays with the bustling modern scene. You can look across the square to the Cross Foxes Inn at which literary celebrity Mrs Piozzi-better known as Mrs Thrale, the friend of Dr Johnson, used to stay when she came to Prestatyn for sea bathing and the salubrious air 120 years ago. The latest films are shown in a cinema that faces the shapely Penisardre farmhouse that dates from Elizabethan times. The beach of firm golden sand which stretches for miles in either direction is ideal for walks and picnics and children of all ages find it a paradise, sand castle building, donkeys, ice cream kiosks, Pierrots, and a café for refreshments are there for their diversion."*

The picture above, also a 1930s view, shows the prestigious one thousand seater Palladium cinema built in 1921 (see page 35 - where Boots the chemist is today). In subsequent years, the Palladium drew vast audiences and for the price of a cinema ticket in the 1920s of nine pence (4 1/2p), one shilling and sixpence (8p) or two shillings and four pence (12p), a uniformed male usher led cinema-goers up the marble stepped entrance and on admission, female usherettes showed them to a carpeted cinema with tip-up seating, rather elegant in the days when most cinemas of the day where known as *"flea pits"* or the *"laugh and scratch"*.

One of the very first films shown at the Palladium was The Shark (silent) advertised as *"a thrilling sea story"*. The Palladium which had a strong sense of belonging to the town was demolished long before its time in 1978. The oak trees stand on land where 16th century Penisardre farmhouse once stood, an important and valuable legacy to the town, sadly demolished in 1964. To protect our future, we must learn from the past, but do we ever?

A brief history of Rhyl Carnival

One of the most important, valuable and prestigious events in Rhyl's historic rich past, thankfully still going strong and continuing to delight is the pomp, ceremony and colour that is Rhyl Carnival, which originated to draw people together both young and old alike, and to help stimulate trade and attract visitors. Starting with the very first Rhyl Carnival on Friday May 1st 1891 (then known as May Day) with Beta Barger having the honour of being Rhyl's first Carnival Queen. Not only has the crowning of the Queen been one of the most notable and integral Rhyl events in each succeeding year, the carnival has also uplifted the town and given pleasure, enjoyment and a sense of belonging to the children and the people of Rhyl. During the carnival's early years, excursion trains were run to the town from different parts of North Wales, transporting vast numbers to see the biggest and most illustrious carnival in Wales, in the days when the Carnival Queen was crowned on the promenade near the Queens Hotel.

Today the Carnival Queen is crowned at the Town Hall. When Rhyl's very first Carnival Queen Beta Barger was being crowned on the promenade in 1891 by Percy Pratt of Brynllithrig Hall, he commented "I am sure I could not be asked to crown a fairer Queen not only in North Wales but the whole of Great Britain, you could not have selected a bonnier more beautiful queen than she who sits in this chariot of honour. I hope that she may live long and that every Queen that may be crowned in Rhyl will be as bonny as this one" Following the placing of a floral crown on her head Beta Barger was subsequently presented with a bible. There has been a panorama of changing times, values and fashions since the first Rhyl Carnival in 1891, in the days when there were no motor cars only horse driven vehicles, and the procession which commenced from the Town Hall was two miles long numbering 250 entries parading the streets.

In 1891 the sixteen competitive classes for prizes were offered for the best horse drawn milk cart, landau, wagonette and omnibus. The winner received twenty shillings (£1) and the smartest postman on parade received a prize of five shillings

(25p). Nothing as colourful had ever been seen in Rhyl before than that of the 1891 carnival, and it was said that with so many people passing to and fro and crossing the procession no accident or injury occurred on the day, The Rhyl Carnival took a temporary break in 1897 for Queen Victoria's Jubilee and also during the four years from 1916 to 1920.

Since then many carnivals have come and gone and it has flourished to the spectacular and colourful event it is today. But almost throughout the entire history of Rhyl Carnival one name has been prominent, that of Palkinghorn. Before the early 1900s Mr J.D. Palkinghorn was an active member of the carnival committee and took over as secretary in 1906 until his death in 1930. The entire Palkinghorn family has taken a lifelong interest in the Rhyl Carnival as far back as 1899. Another name which was synonymous with the carnival was that of Fred Henson, who became Carnival Chairman in 1929. The carnival was at on time held in May and subsequently referred to as "May Day". In later years it was held in July and has since been known as Carnival Day. A spectacular and illustrious event ablaze with colour that embraces an assemblage and a collaboration which involves; local schools, nursing homes, nurseries, local groups and organisations, bands and emblazoned floats, majorettes, dancing troupes and a parade of carnival queens from neighbouring towns as far a field as Liverpool and Manchester, followed by a host of competitions and displays on the carnival field. The first Miss Rhyl was Louvain Evans in 1933, and this prestigious honour is still very much an important and a principal element of Rhyl Carnival today. It must be said that a team of carnival committee volunteers work tirelessly around the year to stage Rhyl Carnival's success. Let us be hopeful that the sun shines on subsequent Rhyl Carnivals as glorious as every carnival has been since 1891, and that they also bring many sublime memories to what is after all a valuable part of Rhyl's heritage rich tapestry of colour.

Opposite page: Woodburns Sewing Factory, Cefndy Road, Rhyl who won first prize for Best Carnival Float in 1969. Pictured are Susan Jones, Violet Roberts, Megan Jones, Lynn Parry, Kathy Harrison, Jeanette Clark, Clare Bando, Sandra Fox & Sandra Williams.
Above left: Rhyl Carnival Procession 1935 in Queen Street. Carnival Queen Eileen Dorothy May Jones and her retinue are pictured on the float.
Above right: Miss Rhyl 1944 Patricia Hodnett being crowned. Looking on is Mayor Dave Rogers.

Carnival days

Bands, dancing troupes, decorative and colourful floats, competitions, displays, hours of hard work behind the scenes by dedicated volunteers, and hopefully a guest appearance from the sun – yes, it's that time of the year again when one of the oldest, largest and most popular events in North Wales, Prestatyn Carnival continues to delight with its customary annual pomp, ceremony, colour and ambience.

The beginnings of Prestatyn Carnival date back to 1919/1921 as a celebration of peace that followed the First World War (see page 40 of my book Memory Lane Volume I for Prestatyn's carnival history). Throughout the 1920s, sand modelling on the foreshore and baby shows at the National School Building, Bastion Road, were incorporated in the carnival week and become a very popular carnival event, with first prize of five shillings (25p) for children under ten and ten shillings (50p) for fourteen to sixteen year olds in sand modelling and an open competition for the best model of Rhuddlan Castle. In the baby show competitions, there were first prizes of a silver cup for babies up to six months and second prizes of ebony and silver hair brushes for babies up to three years of age; for babies twelve months to two years, there was a first prize of a silver knife, fork and spoon in a case, and a second prize of a shantung silk frock. Happy days indeed!

Above left: Frances Humphries having just won first prize for this costume in the Best Comic Impersonator at Prestatyn's 1923 Carnival.
Above right: Crowds line Prestatyn High Street for the town's 1929 Carnival. Malcolm Campbell's Bluebird had recently broken the Land Speed Record at 300mph. The Bluebird seen here was built by Albert Hobbs from cardboard boxes on a wooden frame over a real car.
Left: Eluned Williams looking intoxicatingly pretty as 1924 Prestatyn Carnival Queen.